# QUALITY CIRCLES IN SCHOOLS: A GUIDE TO PROBLEM SOLVING

## DR DHEERAJ MEHROTRA

Copyright © Dr Dheeraj Mehrotra
All Rights Reserved.

ISBN 979-888606597-8

This book has been published with all efforts taken to make the material error-free after the consent of the author. However, the author and the publisher do not assume and hereby disclaim any liability to any party for any loss, damage, or disruption caused by errors or omissions, whether such errors or omissions result from negligence, accident, or any other cause.

While every effort has been made to avoid any mistake or omission, this publication is being sold on the condition and understanding that neither the author nor the publishers or printers would be liable in any manner to any person by reason of any mistake or omission in this publication or for any action taken or omitted to be taken or advice rendered or accepted on the basis of this work. For any defect in printing or binding the publishers will be liable only to replace the defective copy by another copy of this work then available.

# Contents

# Preface

*Quality Circles in Schools is a priority towards quality learning and teaching in particular. The concept of Quality Circles began in Japan and with the march of the time celebrated its importance globally. Not only in manufacturing units but for sure it has reached schools globally. Now the format of quality circles has reached schools and in classrooms where the students and teachers use it as a tool for problem-solving and innovating creative ideas and implement the same towards their work-life to attain success at large. I am sure the readers shall find a novel way of learning through this book.*

*Best & Cheers*

*Dr Dheeraj Mehrotra*

*www.authordheerajmehrotra.com*

# CHAPTER ONE

# QUALITY IN ACADEMICS

**Education** is the process of getting knowledge. It is a must for every human being, no matter which part of the globe he belongs. It is the basis of creating a civilised society. Education and literacy are two different things. Being literate means being capable of reading and writing, while education provides the capability to reason. Every country invests in the best deal in making its citizens educated. Education helps a person earn an excellent living, live a luxurious life and become the best human being. After clothing, food and shelter, education has become critical. Educated citizens form the backbone of every rising economy. The following points highlight the importance of quality in schools in an individual's life.

## It helps in earning an excellent living.

Best legal education is a must to earn a top paying job. If you own a business, being educated supports you to think about new ways to take your business forward. Education provides you with financial independence and helps you afford a comfortable life.

## Education helps in building a better society.

Man is known as a social animal. Education teaches him many things like basic etiquette, regulations, rules and ways to behave with others. It supports building a society of civilised people working for the advantage of each other. Educated citizens can differentiate between what is wrong and right. They *are alert of their fundamental duties and rights and follow laws governing the country.*

### It brings confidence

*Education supports in building self-confidence. It provides you with the capability to make informed decisions and helps in communicating thoughts to others in an effective and better way.*

### It supports in contributing to the nation's economy

**Education plays a vital role in taking the economy forward. An economically independent and educated society is an asset to every country.**

### It raises reasoning capability.

*The most significant advantage that education brings is to support people reason against the illogical. It helps fight against the superstitions that uneducated people or else follow blindly. Educated people can think sensibly and make arguments based on scientific reasoning. It keeps you alert of the new happenings and development around the globe and helps in keeping pace with evolving technology. It provides you with an excellent understanding of the things happening around you. Hence I propose to the masses, Learning to Learn must be a hobby rather than an occasional occurrence in particular.*

*Dr Ushavati Shetty, Principal, Navodaya English High School & Jr. College, Thane, Maharashtra, shares about the school teaching and learning as:*

*Balak ( child)- Palak (parent)-Chalak (school) - Collaborative Leadership Trio!!!!*

*The school lays a strong foundation for a community, a society, a nation and even the world.*

*Lesson planning by the educator should begin with "Student" as a learner in mind as against the curriculum artefact; this will help shorten the distance between the student and their understanding levels, thereby allowing us to bridge the teaching-learning gap that has been widened all thanks to the Pandemic. It places students at the centre of the learning process.*

*Encouraging parent engagement is more than common courtesy in today's times and has always been so. It's one of the best ways to create a positive learning environment for every student. While teachers can advise parents on some things, parents also have essential information about their child that teachers might not know. Both can bring perspectives to the table to enrich a student's learning experience. Neither is complete without the other. A significant impediment to becoming involved for many parents is lack of time. Working parents are often unable to attend school events or meetings during the day. When parents and teachers work together to establish a thriving classroom, the effect on their students is profound. It's often noticed in Indian scenarios that mothers are more involved in their child's academic development.*

*In my experience as a teacher, most of the fathers don't even know which division their child studies in the school if asked. Fathers, like mothers, play a vital role in young children's lives. Children do better educationally, psychologically and socially when fathers are actively involved in their child's schooling years.*

*When parents can get involved, their participation can help schools make the most of existing resources. And there are many ways for parents to stay involved in their children's education that does not require a trip to the school. The more parents are involved in their children's education, the better it is for their entire educational years.*

*Coming together is a beginning. Keeping together is progress. Working together is a success. The ratio of We's to I's is the best indicator of the development of any team. Alone we can do so little; together, we can do so much!*

*Let's not confine our children to our learning, for they were born in another time !!!! Children have never been very good at listening to their elders, but they have never failed to imitate them. An example is not the main thing in influencing students; It is the only thing. Let's set an inspiring example!*

The less you
talk, the mor
time you hav

9

# CHAPTER TWO

# QUALITY CIRCLES IN ACADEMICS

*Quality Circle is a group of members who get together in a circle and sit and brainstorm over a work-related problem; they analyse, identify and discuss strategies and solutions towards its implementation. The history*

*of Quality Circles is related to JAPAN as the first country to have introduced this concept for its workers. It was more like a voluntary activity to identify the work-related problems and develop solutions to the same through various tools of Quality Circle methodology.*

*With the introduction of this quality philosophy, the country rose like a phoenix after the devastation of the second world war. The practice of this concept under the umbrella of KAIZEN gave pace to monitoring the quality practices and development of the nation.*

*QC in Academics has had its pace through the introduction of Quality Circles during the early 1990s' with the inspiration of Quality Enthusiast, Dr Jagdish Gandhi, who introduced the idea of Quality on his return from Japan Circles in his school at City Montessori Schools, Lucknow, in India. Dr Vineeta Kamran, one of the heads of his schools, along with the help of P.C.Bihari and S. Das, introduced this concept as a practice towards learning and teaching in classrooms ever since the idea of Quality Circles became a craze for schools towards excellence as a joint initiative.*

*Slowly and steadily, the concept enriched the interest of school leaders in other countries too. The schools from Nepal, Sri Lanka, Mauritius, UK, USA, Pakistan and Bangladesh took the lead through the First International Convention On Students' Quality*

*Circles, way back in 1997 at Lucknow, India.*

*Ever since the inception of Quality Circles has garnered priority within schools, and NEPAL has introduced it as a subject in their school curriculum to the surprise of many. This has been one of the revolutionary steps to promote the cause and concern towards Quality Awareness within schools.*

*The year 2017 celebrated two decades of this concept within schools, through the participation of over 500 delegates at the 20th International Convention on Students' Quality Circles- 2017, which was organised from 14th to 19th May, at Embilipitiya, Sabaragamuwa Province of Sri Lanka, in collaboration with the Ministry of Education, Information Technology & Cultural Affairs and Department of Education. The convention's theme was " Students' Quality Circles as an Integral Part of Total Quality Management in Education." It proved to be an excellent opportunity for the students, teachers, principals and quality enthusiasts to build knowledge of each others' country, people, culture and language and acquire global awareness and skills so crucial to living and working in the worldwide village, creating long-life friendships across cultures, rightly commented by Herath P. Kularathna, Chief Secretary-Sabaragamuwa Province, & Director General (WCTQEE), Sri Lanka.*

*The chief minister of the host nation, Mahiepala Herath, of the recently concluded ICQC, quotes on importance of Quality Circles, "I strongly believe that this convention brings the students from different cultures, regions, religions, languages and colour to come under a single umbrella to make a single globe by sharing and exchanging their views, ideas and knowledge and will provide an opportunity to students of different countries to compete on a common platform which will strengthen the understanding and communication among youths from different countries, promoting friendship around the world and cultivating the spirit of teamwork and cooperation."*

*The convention did prove to be an excellent nurturing platform for the student delegates who participated actively in various activities, including the "Quality Circles Case Study Presentations" by the groups. The Quality Circle concept in academics plays a vital role in the overall development of the students with a wide range of learning spectrum in the process. The kaizen philosophy of continuous improvement is the cult behind the QC concept, and the initiative is to cure ignorance as to the ultimate objective among the students.*

*As discussed above, a Quality Circle is a group of people who assemble in the form of a circle and brainstorm over a particular topic belonging to their work area and try discussing the strategies, causes and solutions and accordingly try implementing it for an answer.*

*A Student Quality Circle, also known as SQC, is a group of 5 to 15 student members; an ideal number is 8, who sit together in a circle and discuss work-related problems. Accordingly, they evaluate the causes of the selected issue, try to solve the same using the various quality tools, and finally develop strategies to plan and execute the derivatives.*

*Steps required to frame a Student Quality Circle:*

*Formation of a group of 5 to 15 members.*

*Selection of the Leader of the Group.*

*Nomenclature of the Group.*

*Facilitator/ Teacher/ Advisor of the group*

*Brainstorming Sessions*

*Periodic Meetings*

*Issues being discussed.*

*Selection of the problem.*

*Identification and Review of the problem.*

*Identification of the Causes of the selected problem.*

*Implementing TOOLS of problem-Solving.*

*Evaluation of the Case Study.*

*Development of Strategies.*

*Implementation of Strategies.*

*Sharing/ Observation of outcomes.*

*The scenario of Quality Circles frame the inception and implementation through a process of mainly three to four months and may re-occur with the frame to take another problem or concern by the group. In every change of project objective, it is recommended that the leadership changes from one member to the other. Ideally, the number should be eight and all should work as a team with an equal share of responsibilities and concerns. Keeping the members' contribution in view, the duties are divided during the case study presentation before the school management/ school assembly, which further promotes the shared objectives and strategies to become a practice for the others to emulate as a norm. The aim is to promote the quality culture of "Making Students Street Smart".*

## *A Priority for Schools:*

### *The Smooth Classroom Management*

*Learning comes through priority teaching via creativity and intelligence by dedicated teachers. The most effective time for pupils to find out about your guidelines is throughout the first day. Also, before courses begin, you would need to understand what to get out of trainees and how they can fulfil those assumptions. So, when describing the class policies on the first day, please make sure that they comprehend them plainly and understand the effects of not following the guidelines. If you stop working to clarify or give penalties or repercussions of going against class guidelines after that, trainees would certainly obtain not track them in any way.*

*Class monitoring describes how educators see to it that lessons proceed despite disturbance. Class monitoring assists educators in managing concerns regarding inspiration, self-control, and regard. Educators utilise various methods and strategies to ensure that their trainees are motivated, inspired, and manner. Indeed, strategies would undoubtedly depend upon the instructor's choice. This is undoubtedly a choice by all educators who tend to deliver quality as a priority by all means.*

*Most instructors would undoubtedly have three tasks in a forty-five min duration. The pupil reach launches their power and at the same time find out something. Suppose your trainees attempt to depart the conversation right into something unnecessary after that, do not state that directly. You can try to attach it and begin to return to the initial subject after that. If your trainees confront that, do not suggest making them concur with you. They will undoubtedly withstand extra if you require them. Allow them to see what are the effects of their harmful practices.*

*One more approach that educators use is making their trainees feel that they take care of them. You might ask exactly how they are whenever you see them. If they are genuinely rowdy, you might draw them out when every person is active and ask them what is incorrect. In some cases, pupils will certainly inform you of some issues they have come across in the house or college. Hence the priority has to be to create a wow learning atmosphere through comic, engagement and recognition via praises to the students at large.*

*A mentor can be challenging if lively and loud trainees will undoubtedly interrupt the lessons. As an educator, maintaining the lectures and conversations rolling might be challenging if you keep obtaining disrupted. This is confirmed to be tough to manage, specifically for those simply beginning in their training career. Here comes the reflection towards engaging kids, emphasising sharing their views via mind maps on the move.*

*If you are having troubles with particular pupils and ending up being way too much for you to manage, do not require it right into on your own. There are many facets of individuals in the institution management that might assist. You can talk with the support counsellor and request any suggestions on exactly how to encounter or manage the concern. If the trainee will undoubtedly coordinate, you can have them satisfy the counsellor themselves.*

*The bottom line is pupils additionally have suppressed power inside them. If extra in their lessons, those power will undoubtedly blow up in various other methods. As an educator, you would need to see that that power is invested in a beneficial way. Educators are not just interested in academic training but also in ensuring that the pupils' ability is taken into favourable and efficient usage.*

*Trainees that often tend to come to be rowdy are pressed right into doing turbulent behaviour since they are tired. It is best to prevent an hour-long lecture. If you remain to do that, your pupils would certainly rest or have fun with their cell phones as well as various other devices. If you observe that it would certainly take a military prior to your trainees can stay strapped in their seats within the following hr after that include various type of tasks.*

*Make it a component of your program or subject curriculum. Go over the regulations, point-by-point if essential. Much in priority like what you perform in scholastic subjects. This would certainly assist clean out any type of misconception and also incorrect analysis.*

## Solution to all problems:

# QUALITY CIRCLES

A Quality Circle is a group
Of 5 to 12 members who
Sit together in the form of
A circle to brainstorm over
A common problem and
Solve the same using tools
Of problem solving.

## Formation of a Quality Circle:

- ❑ Selecting members as a group.
- ❑ Giving a name to the group.
- ❑ Electing a leader
- ❑ Brainstorming over issues
- ❑ Selecting an issue
- ❑ Getting Solutions
- ❑ Setting Strategies
- ❑ Presentation before the Management
- ❑ Feedback & Implementation

# Solving problems (Proposed):

**Cause and Effect Analysis**

- Identifying the Likely Causes of Problems
  *(Also known as Cause and Effect Diagrams, Fishbone Diagrams, Ishikawa Diagrams, Herringbone Diagrams, and Fishikawa Diagrams.)*

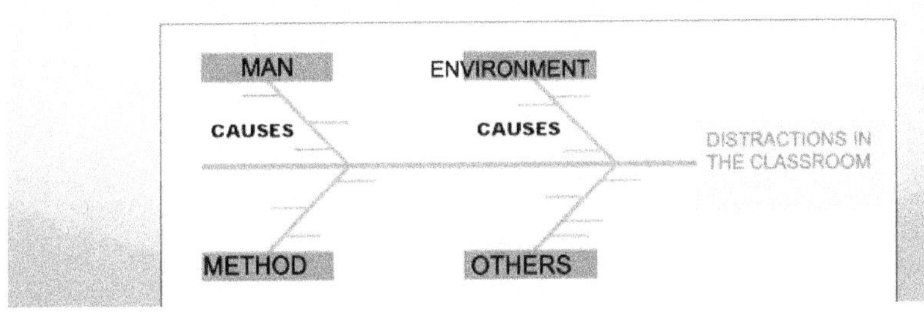


KAIZEN Presentation for Schools by EDUCATORS

By Teams

1. Introduction

2. Problem Identification

3. Explanation of Fish Bone Diagram

4. Strategies

5. Queries by audience

Objective: To ZAP the Audience !!

# Academic Responsibilities

*The Quality Circle (QC) can be used to solve any problem in the school through the process of BRAINSTORMING. The teachers' team up to brainstorm, develop ideas and reflect on them using the FISHBONE DIAGRAM. This further yields the conception of SOLUTION TO THE PROBLEM.*

*The quality of any school is progressed and harnessed via an Academic Process and through this counts the measure of the annual curriculum plan in particular.*

*1. Preparing the Book List, with changes, if any, Syllabus and Curriculum: This defines the approach of managing the books, changes if any. I am planning the syllabus and designing and drafting the curriculum.*

*2. Setting and organising the Split up Plan: To define and drive the best out of planning and executing the plan.*

*3. Assuring the Systematic Coverage of Syllabus as per Split up Plan: This must be modified and followed with the proper spectrum and follow up in the documentation.*

4. *Developing the Chapterwise weightage: This is defined as a priority with learning outcomes related to micro-teaching done, if any, with the classes by the teachers.*

5. *Stress and Focus on Learning become a priority and have to be given a task to execute with the support of the parents and the other teachers teaching in the class.*

6. *Focus on Development of Competencies: Here, the competencies include teaching by the teacher and learning by the students.*

7. *Stress on concept clarity: This defines a published outcome for standard class delivery by the teachers/ Head of Departments while they inspect or observe the classes in practice.*

8. *Regular HW assignments and corrections reflect the learning style and assessment.*

*9. Workbook practices through the guidelines via the spectrum as suggested and referred by the respective boards of examination/ local bodies/ NCF/ NEP and others.*

*10. Work Sheets and their evaluation after completion of a Chapter. This must be monitored and recorded with a preface towards benchmarking test papers and sample papers drafted and suggested by the boards/ council.*

*11. The Rapport is moduled via a proper communication channel. Hence, Communication to students about content/portion of Syllabus before Test/Exam and relative guidelines in the preface to making the best in given time and conformity towards timely course completion and checking of the notebooks.*

*12. Provision of Revision schedule before test and assessment.*

*13. Exploring a Report on syllabus coverage in the review meeting as a priority.*

*14. Making the Performance Assessment Test and Exam Schedule with interactive assessment.*

*15. Framing the Question paper blueprint, Setting of Question Paper, Marking Scheme and Answerkey and the due revision milestone chart.*

*16. Compilation of Results, Progress Report, Descriptors and a follow up with the parents.*

*17. Assuring and Scheduling the PTM, discussing results with parents, and documenting the feedback.*

*18. On priority with feedback mechanism through the Documentation of the Feedback from Parents.*

*19. Making an action plan, assuring that the Action was taken reports on the feedback of parents snd communicating to the stakeholders.*

*20. Finish the marking and complete the Students'*

*Attendance Register.*

*21. Assure and document all the Communication with the parents about HW through the student diary.*

*22. Developing a planned and the execution of the Lesson planning and regular submission of the Teacher's diary.*

*23. Assignment of the Conduct Test as per schedule.*

*24. Prepare and distribute Progress Report.*

*25. Analyse and Submit the feedback reports of parents after PTM.*

*26. Defining the vision and the mission.*

*37. Making learning a priority for all the stakeholders in particular.*

# CHAPTER FOUR

# MANAGING CLASSROOMS EFFECTIVELY

*The spectrum of Learning, Teaching and the Teacher's outlook is explored to the best of priority in*

*totality. The cloud computing Scenario activates the connectivity with pride to learn/ share/ collaborate and blend the learning teaching outlook within schools. The innovative learning is not limited to a physical space but an open learning scenario with a preface to one's comfort at his reading home at home or a TV room at large. It is very much unlike the classroom learning with the same group all days, all the time. Here the community is different and the learning is more spectacular further.*

## RESEARCH OBJECTIVE

*The objective of this study is to evaluate the learning methodology through the inception of cloud computing as one of the quality variables to learning.*

## RESEARCH INITIATIVE

*The paper modules the activation of technology towards High Achieving results and beneficiary satisfaction among schools. The inertia is towards making learning happen within the new age classrooms via the cloud connect where schools and colleges libraries and the teachers, in particular, have not much of dependence for knowledge delivery with the expansion queues to the students at large, with the framework of TECH CANDIES AND APPROACHES being made available at length.*

*The connectivity via the cloud community is great and to the reach of the majority. It certainly sounds funny to some but the fact remains to betray us that the very Indian Education System is one of the unique curriculum facets in the country at par with the developing ones. It is good and one of the flourishing with the march of developing a culture of WWW (Whatever, When Ever and Wherever) force of learning phase by the masses. Our learners today are SMART, viz. Systematic, Meticulous, Artistic, Realistic and Tactful towards getting the right kind of education. We are utilizing the talents of an excellent knowledge base and culture of Learning by doing. No doubt, the implementation of ICT based learning shall give a fillip to the required expertise in a big way. The limitations appear at random but certainly reflect the dynamic ideas and opportunities via investments towards infrastructure, knowledge hubs and teaching skills. We look forward to a knowledge hub in the country giving pace to foreign Universities soon. What is needed is a knowledge society integrated with a guild of Learners and Lectures at a common wavelength of learning and delivering the knowledge.*

## *RESEARCH OUTCOME*

*The study allows the delivery of new order learning for our children explores the intelligence with teachers in demand of being a ROCKSTAR. The application of novel modules integrated with multimedia based packages/ contents is applicable to the new learning for our 21st Century Googlers. The Indian Scenario of Academic climate of schools has had a remarkable sense of change and modularity through the introduction of CCE in particular and it has been rightly nurtured via the Mentor/ Mentee research-based delivery by the Central Board of Secondary Education. What I believe in a sense is the change that needs to be mustered. As a matter of fact, we must believe in the fact that Learning should be just that, not memorization of content provided by the instructor which limits people who have different learning styles (auditory, visual, kinesthetic etc.) to assimilate the information. Above all the Indian learning scenario needs to be focused on an outcome, not THE outcome of the result allowing for different perspectives of thought and internalization of the subject. Taking it one step further is the collaborative model which incorporates a team on a "hunt" for information forming a conclusion based on personal land shared perspective (synthetic learning) highly desired today.*

*The promotion in the case of implementing the new tools of learning has yielded in generating the Quality cult in schools of today with a spectrum of inputs through the stakeholders viz. Parents, Students and the teachers. As a matter of fact, it is true to the world that the teachers are no longer the sole imparters of knowledge but they need to empower the students to learn at a pace and at their leisure through personal learning networks keeping their special traits of talents and interests. The teachers just don't end up after the class is over but on the jolt for 24 hours around the cyber linkage or social networks further. There is no wall now or the boundary of learning. The innovative educator has to evolve a personal learning network for his or her improvement first. Not only this, it has to reach the students as well wherein there is no boundary of limitation in a big way. It is a way to build ones' own classroom and one's own network of learning. The change or the shift here is that we can connect around and share ideas that are not so in the one to many modes of classroom learning.*

*By doing these types of projects students and teachers explore the following:*

- *Providing access to quality education that is practical, relevant, customised and effective.*

- *Adopt innovative ways (tech-based) to provide faster expansion of opportunities of education to all.*

-

*Explore bridging the gap between education and employability.*

▪

*Promote social equality/economic viability.*

## *References:*

*www.sixsigmaineducation.com*

*https://www.amazon.in/200-Wow-Teaching-Ideas-Excellence/dp/1947988875*

*https://www.udemy.com/learn-creative-teaching-skills/learn/v4/*

*https://www.youtube.com/watch?v=RM4_x_3n31g*

*https://www.slideshare.net/dheerajmehrotra/how-to-be-a-rockstar-teacher*

*http://www.lulu.com/shop/dheeraj-mehrotra/six-sigma-in-education-an-initiative-towards-quality-learning/ebook/product-17430307.html*

*https://www.isixsigma.com/methodology/total-quality-management-tqm/applying-total-quality-management-academics/*

*www.dheerajmehrotra.com*

*http://www.qualitydigest.com/inside/quality-insider-news/implementing-six-sigma-education.html*

*https://www.scribd.com/doc/3961102/Six-Sigma-In-Education-Towards-Quality-Education*

*https://www.amazon.fr/BLOGS-TOWARDS-EXCELLENCE-EDUCATION-replicating/dp/3844328750*

# CHAPTER FIVE

# QUALITY EDUCATION: AN ULTIMATE DESIRE BY PARENTS!

*Quality education is the need of the hour. As a result, at the same time, the boards of education and learning must develop a plan to help schools, teachers, and parents educate children about safe, responsible use of the Internet. For example, encourage schools and families to place computers in shared rooms (such as family rooms, dining rooms, offices or libraries), where children can use the Internet with others around them. And teach children never to share personal information (name, address, telephone, or credit card number) online. This may go a long way in making this a success. The day-to-day activities at the school and the home education will provide a healthy liking for the computer. This is required to foster appropriate Internet use among pre-schoolers and other young children.*

*It is also a debating fact that despite the increasing use of computers in elementary schools, there hasn't been a decrease in the formal teaching of penmanship.*

*The children use just as much paper as before computers became a classroom standard. Hence, one must keep in mind that writing with a pencil involves an equally important set of skills like typing on a keyboard.*

*Exposure to the Internet can help preschoolers and children in the early elementary grades master literacy and other cognitive skills and spur the integration of these skills early in their development. Parents and school leaders who look for online opportunities for younger children can be guides to engaging, age-appropriate content. The Internet can reinforce everyday learning opportunities and be a powerful tool for fostering interaction among adults and young children. It takes much to conduct the new means of knowledge in this regard. The teaching gentry's task must ponder the computing of this sort; they must help teachers, parents, and children use the Internet more effectively for learning. For example, they ought to suggest education-related websites for parents and children to visit together - and give them learning activities to do once they get there. Offer education-related help for students online, like after-school tutoring.*

*Provide teachers with professional development opportunities to help them model effective use of the Internet as a tool for students' learning, including integrating Internet learning with traditional classroom learning. If teacher training takes place outside of regular school hours, offer teachers*

*incentives to participate when possible. If teacher training pulls teachers out of the classroom, parents should know why it is essential to support this professional development. The Internet users to communicate more effectively with parents and students goes a long way to generate interest for all. For instance, launch school district or school websites or publicise websites in newsletters and places where parents are likely to be. Update websites frequently with relevant, timely information. Post exemplary student work online, with teacher commentary explaining why this work meets academic standards. Make websites interactive by soliciting comments or holding public forums about education issues online. Encourage teachers, parents, and students to communicate through email, make their email IDs, and even share offline with that reference to generate pulses of craze and interest in being a netizen. And finally, engage the community. This can be quickly done by holding computer and Internet training classes for parents or hosting convenient opportunities for parents, community leaders, librarians, teachers, and others to talk together about children's use of the Internet. Schools may want to collaborate with libraries, community computing centres, local colleges and universities, and other places offering alternative computers access.*

*Educators and parents have been quite concerned over the years about the possible adverse effects of computers and the Internet on children's desire to interact with others. Unlike television, however, the more interactive, child-controlled nature of some computer software can be conducive to sharing, taking turns and playing games together. Also, the fact lies in the versatile saying that the familiarity and comfort with computers are undoubtedly helpful for daily survival, both in and out of school. The risk associated with this myth comes from placing too much emphasis on the computer as a "must" for children's future welfare. It's better to regard computer use as simply one more experience or tool that can support the development of good old-fashioned learning skills such as reading and writing, thinking logically, and solving and analysing problems. It can also enhance the learning process by allowing children to have experiences not possible without a computer. Ultimately out of the study, it capsules more of the truth to have this machine as a*

*tool rather than an aid for all times. One must utilise its measures as and when required from the children's point of concern.*

## FUTURE SCOPE

*The ultimate is Quality Culture and the Happening things to happen. It counts in a big way to promote the cause of darkness out of the old traditions. It is very easily encapsulated into the minds of the workforce, the users, the public opinion and the masses. IT has paved as the irresistible mantra for SURVIVAL, the capsules for QUALITY CULTURE, the tablet for PROSPERITY at large. Pressing it with the opinion of the masses is that it is a REALITY in practice. The boom of technology is bound to promote and enhance the image of Quality in Education and SOCIETY in a big way. Thinking of SOCIETY, aiming for a future, working for.... Without it, IT has become a JOKE of the day. Kudos' to the necessity ... the ultimate choice in action....by Chance and not by choice.*

*IT is here is stay and mandatory to breathe into......
Regardless of one's career choice, computer hardware
and software knowledge can benefit from how these
components function together. Even if one's job does
not require him to work directly with a computer,
this knowledge may help him envision new ways of
using computers, resulting in a more productive work
environment. This can also lead to career
advancement opportunities. If one thinks this case is
being overstated and computers are not being used
that much, consider this: computers pop up in places
and professions that may seem unlikely.*

# ACHIEVING A STUDENT-DRIVEN CLASSROOM

*The learning has taken its pace to the majority who by chance or tribes are governed by today's Google Generation. Alas, to the say, the teachers are no longer the fountain of knowledge but an artistic adult to manage the classroom discipline.*

*The teachers who motivate, differentiate, make content relevant and leave no student behind are more important than any other factor in particular.*

*Students like the subject only when they like the teacher, hence a directly proportional element within a classroom. The drive by the teacher in the class, with the vocabulary, is signified with the equilibrium of learning together rather than teaching. They say, "Teachers know the best", activates wisdom just in the franchise but in action. The sole reason for this far-fetched approach lies in the nutshell element of an easy method of open knowledge, which is unrestricted, versatile and dual with surprises. The satisfaction and the wow part within classrooms only prevail where there is a taste of "It is in the book, Ma'am, tell us something new!" As a teacher, it is our wisdom to teach the "I can do approach" instead of "I shall try approach", which is universally possible only when we use kind words in the class. Compliment each kid, especially the difficult ones. That might be the only positive thing they hear all day.*

*Activating a student-oriented rather than a task-oriented classroom requires more of a connection and a student relationship. At times apologising to students is a learning moment. If we want kids with character, we must model them with others as character counts. The experiences shared in totality that a genuine apology requires freely admitting fault, fully accepting responsibility, a humbled asking for forgiveness, immediately changing of the behaviour and above all, actively rebuilding the trust. The dose of willingness to explore knowledge is desired rather than sharing content from the book. When students appear crusaders of expertise, teachers need to act like facilitators more than strict disciplinarians. It must be made clear to everyone that there is no expiry*

*date for hunger for learning.*

*Let yearning for knowledge be a priority rather than an occasional occurrence. Also, the teachers must explore the power of curing ignorance as to the chief element of choice in every interaction with the students, teachers, peers and parents. It is never too late to make yourself better; it should be the priority. The segment of reality lies in engaging the children in the class with no fear but intimacy and a feeling of pride both by the students and the teachers at large. To the real concerns, the fear kills the dreams than failure ever will, which should be mounted on priority by the masses. The children should be made to enjoy the classroom session with engagement and knowledge sharing using ICT tools and techniques of the cyber world and making their Online reputation management a reality.*

*Today's students are no longer kids but young adults and hence need recognition as individuals and partners in the learning process. Critical thinking must be one of the prime qualities of the children as it is among the first causes for change, but is a parish in schools- for no other reason than it conditions the mind to suspect the form and function of everything it sees, including the classroom scenario, all what is taught and discussed. As a teacher, it is our prime requisites to make progress visible, adjust grading practices, model desired habits and don't get carried away with the politics of the school, the students and the parents. Hey, the voice violates, the Principal's lobby is rushed for, is there any debating subject rises or fumes up. The school principal is targeted and reassured support to the students, as ever be.*

*To govern and sense student's friendly classroom, the teachers need to check on their share of the day, of some new vocabulary and make a haze to the fact that the students should be held accountable for the number and the quality of questions students ask and pursue during the teaching-learning process. Right from Good Morning Wishing to the, Thank you, children, for the time and share has to be so friendly and empowering to make them take home moments of joy and some attributes to share with their parents. This must be a priority. Teachers need to showcase that they are not perfect and never will be in action. They must take risks with their teaching, and failing must be a part of the learning process. We are facing the Google Generation, which empowers self and is not dependent on either the library or the teacher; fortunately, or unfortunately, I doubt my words too.*

*The beautiful words help our children use a wide range of captivating words in their writings. We must not blame them for their handwriting and knowledge limitation; instead, they must be the part and the parcel of their learning. Also, to create a rapport with the students, the teaching tools in practice by the teachers need to be evaluated concerning the usage during the lesson being appropriate or not. With this, the teacher's subject knowledge, enthusiasm, questioning methods, exposition, and problem-solving related to the multilevel dimension for judging. The teachers as facilitators explore and expose the learning objectives in a big bang way via repartees and the responses generated after every class or via the Parents' Teachers' Meetings on jolt and achievements. Let us conclude the fact that children will love and explore their presence in the classrooms only when given the recognition of individual concerns; teachers must call the kids by their first names keeping them at pace to importance rather than experiencing the only preface with them at the time of the roll calls and that too with referencing through roll numbers.*

*The choice is ours, engage or enrage! Let quality be the taste forever instead of being just an occasional occurrence. The priority must be to create a WOW*

*classroom with the tongue of "You can do wonders", "You can do it!" and above all ", All my students are best of the students, and I am proud of them".*

*Happy Teaching!*

# CHAPTER SEVEN

# The Quality Classroom Culture

*Teaching through technology must be a practise rather than an occasional occurrence, for sure if there has to be a Wow feature within classrooms.*

*As teachers, we must not use technology as a silicon coating but harness the power of technology to connect with our students. No more, it is about copying and pasting, which we have had been doing over the years. As a matter of fact, in a lighter vein, power corrupts politicians, and PowerPoint corrupts the teachers if it has just slides and no explanations. The platform should share for show rather than expecting it to be the only parcel for knowledge delivery for a matter of thought and intelligence. There is a specific need to implement a new way of teaching through technology, and hence a digital pedagogy is required the most. The teachers need to introspect how children may learn in this networked environment. We can't simply take a textbook and deliver it digitally. Instead, they need to explore the power to harness the best via connectivity and creativity to connect.*

*We can't think and re-discover the chalkboard and make it an intelligent board to deliver knowledge. What is required is a novel mindset of love, care and delivery of priorities for our children within classrooms. We ultimately need a different paradigm for teaching, a different pedagogy that talks about creation, control of chaos, connection to correcting, and consumption to creation. The teachers need to change their thinking of using technology in education.*

*For sure, we live in a world of change; There are great tweets each minute great Facebook page views each minute. The academic Donald Norman describes skeuomorphism as cultural constraints: interactions with a system learned only through culture. The time which intensifies the tech world with pride. The world has only been used in the tech industry for a few years, where its meaning has changed, says Dan O'Hara, an academic at Birmingham City University. "Skeumorphs are not strictly something that can be designed," he says. "They occur unintentionally when aesthetic styles are inherited without thinking." The photo views of Flickr, which mounts to n' undefined, explore the universal learning of repute. Each minute of over 47,000 app downloads on the apple store encapsulates a new phase of dimensional learning taking place out of the hunger for knowledge. Of course, all these facts did not exist before 2004 by any chance. The availability of data online fascinates the new learner in multiple ways who tend to be a multitasker in pave to grab the unknown. To sound far-fetched but true, the schools over the years have not changed. They have taken the same task as rows and columns with a teacher at pace. They typically, at large, have no technology; hence there has been no change. There are reports too, "Failed iPad Experiment Shows BYOD Belongs in Schools.", "LA. Cancels iPads-in-the-schools program: a failure of vision, not technology. Despite all our heavy investments at schools, it appears there is a failure of our strategy or the idea to implement the best of technology in education.*

*And above all, it seems the inability of our pedagogy. One of our mistakes as educators is CTRL + C & CTRL + V. Necessarily as COPY and PASTE for this can't solve the concerns but expands the issue in particular. This is one of the mistakes we get to govern while implementing technology in our schools.*

*Similarly, the conclusion fetches the scenario of apparent reasons related to shifting the teaching into a new realm. The core teaching principles having a shift need an activated model to conclude without looking back in perfection. The teachers need to be an advocate for holistic education. This transforms the learners in a big way to assist learning and make it happen within the classrooms. Teachers need to keep things simple and do what works for them. For us, the teachers cannot teach the way we were taught. Above all, the students, at large, would only like the subject if they like the teacher, and this is one of the solitaire truths for any holy classroom in particular. Teachers need to have a wellness routine planning sheet, getting the win-win approach of the happiness index of the students, roll number wise. Indeed, classroom management has been identified as a primary concern for teachers, and if they don't get along with the learners as bosses or clients with affection, the management of the class appears as slang.*

*The teachers in the majority have a wrong notion that classroom management is much to do with discipline only and is limited to the children being quiet in the class. In contrast, the goals include identifying misconceptions about managing the teaching, the students and the consequences. The age teachers need to broaden the very conception of classroom management and ultimately provide a framework for developing their classroom management plan. Engaging the children in instructions often leads to classroom management but only a classic time. There has to be a thoughtful physical environment for an activated classroom supported by establishing caring relationships and implementing engaging instructions.*

# CHAPTER EIGHT

# Teaching Mindfulness Towards Excellence in Schools!

*We, the majority, often wonder and ponder over the fact that mindfulness is only beneficial for adults because it is only adults who can feel stress. But contrary to popular belief, stress can affect children, especially in school. Our students experience toxic stress every single day due to pressure to get good grades, an increasingly competitive environment and also the uncertainty of the future.*

*Mindfulness is a condition where the mind is fully aware of what's happening in the present moment, which can be achieved through meditation. It might seem trivial, but mindfulness is essential for a person's mental state because it helps the mind focus on what is currently going on without judging whether it is good or bad.*

*This is why practising mindfulness is not only crucial for adults but also children. Teaching mindfulness in school is crucial to helping students cope with the stress due to the pressures they experience in school. Here are some benefits of mindfulness meditation for students to help them achieve excellence in learning.*

*Improve Attention in Class*

*It is not a secret that many students find it hard to pay attention and concentrate. Surprisingly, laziness is not the real reason for this situation. In most cases, stress, worries, fears and personal problems take their focus away from the lessons.*

*This is where mindfulness meditation will play its role. Practising mindfulness can help students concentrate better because it directly influences the brain, especially the hippocampus part. And since it jogs the hippocampus to be more active, their memory and critical learning skills will improve and help them get better grades.*

*The competition and pressure to always be the best in class can affect the student's social and emotional skills.*

*They tend to only focus on themselves and don't care about what's happening around them.*

*Interpersonal skill is essential to survive in the real world. So, the school must make sure that the pressure to perform well will not harm their interpersonal skills. Mindfulness training will also make the prefrontal cortex, the part of the brain that regulates emotion, more active. As a result, the students will be more empathetic, more pleasant, and improve their behaviour in school.*

*It is usual for students to experience stress when facing a challenging time in their education. However, the situation of the modern education system often forces the students to experience toxic stress, the kind of stress that can negatively affect their mental health.*

*Stress is every day, but it can be dangerous when the students don't know how to deal with the stress. This is one of the main issues that mindfulness practice can solve. Mindfulness helps students see things more objectively and relax their bodies and mind when facing a stressful situation.*

*School should not only focus on lessons and grades, but also education for life. The education system should start to pay attention to the student's mental state too, and mindfulness meditation is one of the best methods. It will teach the students to be more mindful of the present, which can help them cope with stress, improve their optimism about life, and improve their performance in school.*

*Schools predict and practice innovative ways to deliver passion to the students. The yoga sessions and other mind-based exercises reveal an open spectrum of the level of mindfulness we need in our schools today.*

# CHAPTER NINE

# THE PRIORITY LEARNING

*As teachers, we must not use technology as a silicon coating but harness the power of technology to connect with our students. No more, it is about copying and pasting what we have been doing over the years. For control corrupts politicians, so PowerPoint corrupts the teachers with just slides and no explanations. For a matter of thought and intelligence, the platform should share for show rather than expecting it to be the only parcel for knowledge delivery. There is a specific need to implement a new way of teaching through technology, and hence a digital pedagogy is required the most. The teachers need to introspect how children may learn in this networked environment. We can't simply take a textbook and deliver it digitally somewhat. The need here is to explore the power to harness the best via connectivity and creativity to connect.*

*The delivery of new order learning for our children explores the intelligence with teachers in demand of being a ROCKSTAR. The application of novel modules integrated with multimedia based packages/ contents applies to the new learning for our 21st Century Googlers. The Indian Scenario of the Academic climate of schools has had a remarkable sense of change and modularity through the introduction of CCE. It has been rightly nurtured via the Mentor/ Mentee research-based delivery by the Central Board of Secondary Education. What I believe in a sense is the change that needs to be mustered. We must think that Learning should be just that, not memorisation of content provided by the instructor, which limits people who have different learning styles (auditory, visual, kinesthetic etc.) to assimilate the information. Above all, the Indian learning scenario needs to be focused on an outcome, not THE outcome of the result, allowing for different perspectives of thought and internalisation of the subject. The collaborative model takes it one step further, which incorporates a team on a "hunt" for information forming a conclusion based on personal land shared perspective (synthetic learning) highly desired today.*

*The promotion in the case of implementing the new tools of learning has yielded in generating the Quality cult in schools of today with a spectrum of inputs through the stakeholders viz. Parents, Students and the teachers. Indeed, the teachers are no longer the sole imparters of knowledge. Still, they need to empower the students to learn at a pace and leisure through personal learning networks to keep their unique talents and interests. The teachers don't end after the class is over but on the jolt for 24 hours around the cyber linkage or other social networks. There is no wall now or the boundary of learning. The innovative educator has to evolve a personal learning network for improvement first. Not only this, it has to reach the students as well, wherein there is no boundary of limitation in a big way. It is a way to build ones' classroom and one's learning network.*

**We can't think and re-discover the chalkboard and make it a smartboard to deliver knowledge. What is required is a novel mindset of love, care and delivery of priorities for our children within classrooms. We ultimately need a different paradigm for teaching, a different pedagogy that talks about creation, control of chaos, connection to correcting and above all, consumption to creation. The teachers need to change their thinking of how they will use technology in education.**

*The availability of data online fascinates the new learner in multiple ways who tend to be a multitasker in pave to grab the unknown. To sound far-fetched but true, the schools over the years have not changed. They have taken the same task as rows and columns with a teacher at pace. They typically at large have no technology; hence there has been no change. There are reports too, "Failed iPad Experiment Shows BYOD*

*Belongs in Schools.", "LA. Cancels iPads-in-the-schools program: a failure of vision, not technology. Despite all our heavy investments at schools, it appears there is a failure of our strategy or the idea to implement the best of technology in education. And above all, it seems the inability of our pedagogy. One of our mistakes as educators is CTRL + C & CTRL + V. Necessarily as COPY and PASTE for this can't solve the concerns but expands the issue in particular. This is one of the mistakes we get to govern while implementing technology in our schools.*

*Similarly, the conclusion fetches the scenario of obvious reasons, which relate to shifting the teaching into a new realm. The core teaching principles having a shift need an @ctivated model to conclude with the no looking back in perfection. The teachers need to be an advocate for holistic education. This transforms the learners in a big way to assist learning and make it happen within the classrooms. Teachers need to keep things simple and do what works for them. For us, the teachers, cannot teach the way we were taught. Above all, the students, at large, would only like the subject if they like the teacher, and this is one of the solitaire truths for any holy classroom in particular. Teachers need to have a wellness routine planning sheet, getting the win-win approach of the happiness index of the students, roll number wise. Indeed, classroom management has been identified as a primary concern for teachers, and if they don't get along with the learners as bosses or clients with affection, the management of the class appears as slang. The teachers in the majority have a wrong notion that classroom management is much to do with discipline only and is limited to the children being quiet in the class. In contrast, the goals include identifying misconceptions about managing the teaching, the students and the consequences. The teachers of age need to broaden the very conception of classroom management and ultimately provide a framework for developing their classroom management plan. Engaging the children in instructions often leads to classroom management but only a classic time. For having an activated classroom, there has to be a thoughtful physical environment supported by establishing caring relationships and implementing engaging instructions.*

# CHAPTER TEN

# CLASSROOM QUALITY TRAITS

*Learning is a process that is attained primarily by teaching via creativity and intelligence by dedicated teachers. The most effective moment to allow pupils to find out about your guidelines is the very first day. Prior to courses beginning, you would certainly need to understand what to get out of learners as well as just how they can fulfil those assumptions. When describing the class policies on the very first day, make certain that they comprehend them plainly and also understand the impact of not following the guidelines. If you stop working to clarify or give penalties or repercussions of going against class guidelines, learners would certainly assume ways not to follow them.*

## Class Monitoring

*Class monitoring describes just how educators see to it that lessons proceed despite disturbances. Class monitoring assists educators to manage concerns regarding inspiration, self-control and also respect. There are various methods and also strategies that educators utilize to make certain that their learners are motivated, inspired and also mannerly. Certainly, strategies would depend upon the instructor's choice. This is a choice by all educators who tend to deliver quality as a priority by all means.*

## Every Action has a Reaction

*The majority of instructors, usually have 3 tasks in a forty-five minutes duration. The pupil reach launches their power as well as at the exact same time find out something. If your learners are attempting to depart the conversation right into something totally unnecessary after that, do not state that directly. You can attempt to attach it and after that begin to return to the initial subject. If your learners tend to become confrontational, do not insist on agreeing with you. They would certainly withstand extra if you require them. Allow them to see what are the effects of their negative practices.*

## I Care About You

*One more approach that educators use is making their learners feel cared. You can ask a 'how are you whenever you see them. If they are truly rowdy, you might draw them out when every person is busy to ask them if something is wrong. In some cases, pupils will certainly inform you of some issues they have been encountering or struggling with within the house or in school. Hence the priority has to be to create a wow learning atmosphere through comic, engagement and recognition via praises to the students at large.*

## Use a Mind Map

*It can be hard for a teacher to conduct an engaging class with loud learners who tend to interrupt lessons. As an educator, maintaining the lessons as well as conversations rolling might be challenging if the disruption continues. This is confirmed to be tough to manage specifically for those that are simply beginning in their teaching career. Here comes the reflection towards engaging kids with an emphasis on sharing their views via mind maps on the move.*

## Seek a Counsellor Support

*If you are having troubles with particular pupils as well as they are ending up being way too much for you to manage, take help from your school's support counsellor as well as request any type of suggestions on exactly how to encounter or manage the concern. If the trainee will certainly coordinate, you can have them satisfy the counsellor themselves.*

## Utilising Energy of a Learner

*The bottom line is pupils additionally have suppressed energy inside them. That energy, if not utilised during lessons, will certainly blow up in various other ways. As an educator, you would certainly need to see to it that that energy is invested in a beneficial method. Educators are not just interested in scholastic training, however ensuring that the pupils' power is taken into favourable as well as efficient usage.*

## Short but Effective Lecture

*Learners that often tend to come to be rowdy are pressed right into doing turbulent behaviour since they are tired. It is best to prevent an hour-long lecture. If you remain to do that, your pupils would certainly rest or have fun with their cell phones as well as various other devices. If you observe that it would certainly take a military prior to your learners can stay strapped in their seats within the following hr after that include various type of tasks. Make it a component of your program or subject curriculum. Go over the regulations, point-by-point if essential. Much in priority like what you perform in scholastic subjects. This would certainly assist clean out any type of misconception and also incorrect analysis.*

# CHAPTER ELEVEN

# KAIZEN- THE EXPERTISE!

Kaizen is a Japanese term meaning "change for the better" or "continuous improvement." It is a Japanese business philosophy regarding the processes that continuously improve operations and involve all within the organisation. In Academics, the term KAIZEN stands for Quality In Teaching, Learning, Infrastructure and Engagement of Students in the Teaching/ Learning Process.

# CHAPTER TWELVE

# QUALITY CLOUD BASED LEARNING

*Learning is much ado without teaching to preface the spread of knowledge. The teachers today require a CYBER PRESENCE via YouTube videos or a Scribd publication to jelly the taste of engagement with them, the Wi-Fi learners of the new age of but teachers' of any assistance, otherwise.*

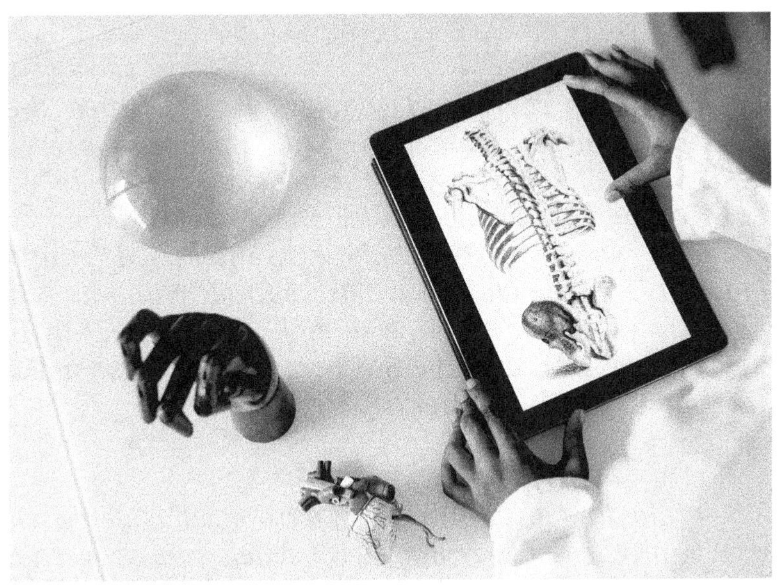

*Cyber based computing has evolved a new era of learning thy way! Via cyberspace at the pace of your own and no definition of the classroom restricted with the four walls of the classroom to be severe and private. Teachers' who once were the SAGE on the STAGE are now forced to be the guides on the floor. They act like facilitators now to students as an aid to learning which is now more a formality in classrooms. Most of the time, he is told the same things that have been already shared with him by their parents/ friends or at the online tutorial option through the various search engines, primarily, the GOOGLE. We encapsulate the very nature of learning, but with a bit of intelligence; otherwise, they come up to us (probably if not, will with the march of time and tide), I quote, "Sir/ Madam, It is already in the book. Please*

*tell us something new". Do we have a reply to them?*

*Various researchers and scholars have defined the need for Quality Education. Still, no one has ever desired the lack of "We" the teachers today to be exciting and "Informed" with the march of time or else we would be the only "Un-interested" thing (Identity) in the class if we are not enriching and of any interest to the children to make them forget their Facebook Walls' and the SMS which otherwise make their mind fertile of interest.*

*The branching of tabs in the classrooms has delivered a new preface of learning, with teachers discovering information and sharing verbatim. Over the years, with the march of time and tide, the education system has delivered progress to the nation and the world as all Top companies globally pay attention and work on the roles of Indians known for their Expertise and Intelligence.*

*The delivery of new order learning for our children explores the intelligence with teachers in demand of being a ROCKSTAR. The application of novel modules integrated with multimedia based packages/ contents applies to the new learning for our $21^{st}$ Century Googlers. The Indian Scenario of Academic climate of schools has had a remarkable sense of change and modularity through the introduction of CCE in particular, and it has been rightly nurtured via the Mentor/ Mentee research-based delivery by the Central Board of Secondary Education. What I believe in a sense is the change that needs to be mustered. We must think that Leerning should be just that, not memorisation of content provided by the instructor, which limits people who have different learning styles (auditory, visual, kinesthetic etc.) to assimilate the information. Above all, the Indian learning scenario*

*needs to be focused on an outcome, not THE outcome of the result, allowing for different perspectives of thought and internalisation of the subject. The collaborative model takes it one step further, which incorporates a team on a "hunt" for information forming a conclusion based on personal land shared perspective (synthetic learning) highly desired today.*

*The promotion in the case of implementing the new tools of learning has yielded in generating the Quality cult in schools of today with a spectrum of inputs through the stakeholders viz. Parents, Students and the teachers. Indeed, the teachers are no longer the sole imparters of knowledge. Still, they need to empower the students to learn at a pace and leisure through personal learning networks, keeping their unique talents and interests. The teachers don't end after the class is over but on the jolt for 24 hours around the cyber linkage or other social networks. There is no wall now or the boundary of learning. The innovative educator has to evolve a personal learning network for improvement first. Not only this, she has to reach the students, wherein there is no boundary of limitation in a big way. It is a way to build ones' classroom and one's learning network. The change or the shift here is that we can connect and share ideas that are not so in the one to many modes of classroom learning.*

*They must be given an opportunity only when required but as a habit to my knowledge and interest. The module, particularly by Next Education India, delivers TeachNext, one of the highly enriched packed e-*

*learning delivery, is entitled to successful learning at large. With over 6,000 schools on the count, the product delivers e-learning with perfection and common interest to the pupils with pride!*

*The innovative learning is not limited to a physical space but an open learning scenario with the preface to one's comfort at his reading home at home or a TV room at large. It is very much unlike the classroom learning with the same group all days, all the time. Here the community is different, and the learning is more spectacular further. Here the teacher concerned is the one who has to be engaged and involved in the conversations as a leader or a facilitator further. And this makes the Indian Education System more challenging to face the 21ˢᵗ Century Learners...who are fertile already with knowledge and come to classrooms to route their intelligence and explore collaborative learning and a Win-Win explore of situations at times.*

*Kudos to the Teachers who are challenged with students arguing towards their favourite replies or responses to their queries in the classrooms. Hopefully, the e-learning or the digital classes help the learning teachers to a limit.*

*Any comments..! Are we prepared. . . Sounds exciting, and we need to prepare for the showcase if we want patient learning to occur in our classrooms.*

# CHAPTER THIRTEEN

# NLP- The Quality Communication Tool

*The Neuro-Linguistic Programming, the NLP derives the essence of learning via*

*Neuro: Which integrates the five senses, Visual, auditory, kinesthetic, olfactory and Gustatory. Visual includes Sights:: Auditory defines sounds we hear:: Kinesthetic defines external feelings like a touch of someone or something:: Olfactory means smell:: Gustatory means taste!*

*Linguistic: Defines the language and other nonverbal communication systems through which our neural representations are coded and include pictures, sounds, feelings, tastes, smells and words.*

*Programming: It is an art to discover and utilise the instructions we run as our communication to ourselves and others to achieve our specific and desired outcomes. It is a tested and progressive model of communicating with ourselves and others. It was initially developed by Richard Bandler, John Grinder and others.*

*The productivity of individuals is explored to the best via the incentives generated of experience and target vision in particular.*

*In academics, as a novice spectrum, the NLP integrates into discovering the art of knowing the students with their level of acceptance and learning in totality. It is like using the language of the mind to consistently achieve our specific and desired outcomes to deliver the knowledge aimed at the students. Based on the teachers' experience in the classrooms, the exploring is delivered via the following:*

*Establishing rapport with an individual student will enable you to help them better and create a win-win situation for everyone.*

*Have a rapport with the group of students by using pacing and leading. Use this to turn the entire group around to your schedule while remaining in charge.*

*Teaching students using the primary senses entails determining the immediate sense system of the student and then delivering information in a way that works best for that system.*

*They are learning how to read students' minds by reading their eye movements.*

*Exploring and identifying the balance between suitable brain days and left brain days. Determining which mode the class is in and then teaching in a manner appropriate to the day's mood in particular.*

*The subjective analysis within the classrooms attracts practical communication skills from teachers and replicates them to the students. The concept integrates the language of the mind to achieve our specific and desired outcomes consistently. The education delivery with excellence after identifying the audience's traits is hence an art being explored via this. This is indeed a great way to facilitate change. It allows us to be in a position wherein there is no concern or a problem. The mindset is a policy here to deliver the best. Some of the ratios which govern this aspect of curing intelligence by educators involve a push, getting out of the comfort zone, shy zone, arranging a massive paradigm shift, discussing the passion, learning to learn from the environment, must feel most alive, need to be happy in your skin, give oneself a round of applause, empower the limiting belief and the negative emotions about self. Classroom teaching is a nourishing talent that crops with the march of time and tide. Behavioural flexibility narrates to the positive outcome only through sensory acuity and psychology excellence.*

*The teaching techniques need to excel with the 'wow' feature with a positive belief by the educators. The nurturing keys to an achievable outcome follow as follows:*

- *Being positive*

- *Specified present situation*

- *Specified outcome*

- *Specified evidence procedure*

- *Self-initiated and self-maintained*

- *Appropriately contextualised*

- *Must be ecological*

*The approaches govern a practical approach to "All I need is within me now !", let the teachers approach students with a say "Raise your hand high and tall and say YES !" to promote the sense of agility and promptness during the sessions. The excellence that we point to activates the six human needs of our students and educators. The activation delivers via Certainty, Uncertainty/ Variety, Love & Connection, Significance, Growth and Contribution. All these replicate to confidence and provide the power to perform. As teachers, we need to abide by the presuppositions of the NLP, which act like convenient assumptions. It is a requisite of desire to respect for the other person's world model; the behaviour and change are to be evaluated in terms of context and Ecology. The resistance in a client (student) is a real sign of a lack of rapport. People (pupils) are not their behaviours; Everyone is doing the best one can with the resources they have available, every behaviour is motivated by positive intent. As a teacher, one has to calibrate on behaviour as the essential information about a person is that person's behaviour.*

*Mirroring in classrooms: As teachers, the Mirroring technique of NLP distinguishes the matching portions of another person's behaviour, as in a mirror. This justifies the learning and the learner and the interest between them.*

*Modelling with children: This is another crucial technique to set the process of learning where we elicit the strategies, filter patterns and physiology that allows someone to produce a specific behaviour. This can be further tackled, modelled and paced as required.*

*Pacing with Children: This activates the conclusion. It delivers the matching or mirroring of another person's external behaviour to gain rapport. The joy with the kids encounter at ease and perforates learning as a resultant.*

*The spectrum of learning for fun gets via this NLP, which suffices to the limitations of dissatisfaction among the masses, particularly the stakeholders viz., the students and the parents. Activating this would undoubtedly result in penetration to learning as a habit rather than an occasional occurrence.*

**<u>References:</u>**

*www.nlpforeducators.com*
*https://yourstory.com/2017/02/a5ef2268e9-nlp-in-academics/*
*https://www.youtube.com/watch?v=wCphVA3dtEg*

# About The Author

www.authordheerajmehrotra.com

Dheeraj Mehrotra has been honoured with the President of India's National Teacher Award in the year 2006 and the Best Science Teacher State Award, Innovation in Education for his inception of Six Sigma In Education by Education Watch, New Delhi and Education World- Best Teacher Award, BOLT Learner Teacher Award by Air India, 'Innovation in Education Award 2016' among others. He has developed over 150 FREE EDUCATIONAL MOBILE Apps for the Google Play Store exclusively for Teachers, Students, and Parents. This work has been recognized by the LIMCA BOOK OF RECORDS & INDIA BOOK OF RECORDS as the only Indian to draw that feast. Dr Mehrotra is presently working as a PRINCIPAL at KUNWARS GLOBAL SCHOOL, Lucknow, in India.

He is an active TEDx speaker. As a premium UDEMY Instructor, he has also developed over 450 courses and is catering to over 8 Lakh students from 180 plus countries.

He can be visited at www.authordheerajmehrotra.com

101
SCHOOL
MANAGEMENT
STRATEGIES
Towards EFFECTIVE
QUALITY MANAGEMENT
System in Schools
DR. DHEERAJ
MEHROTRA

DR. DHEERAJ MEHROTRA
99 EFFECTIVE WAYS
TO MANAGE YOUR SCHOOLS
POST COVID-19

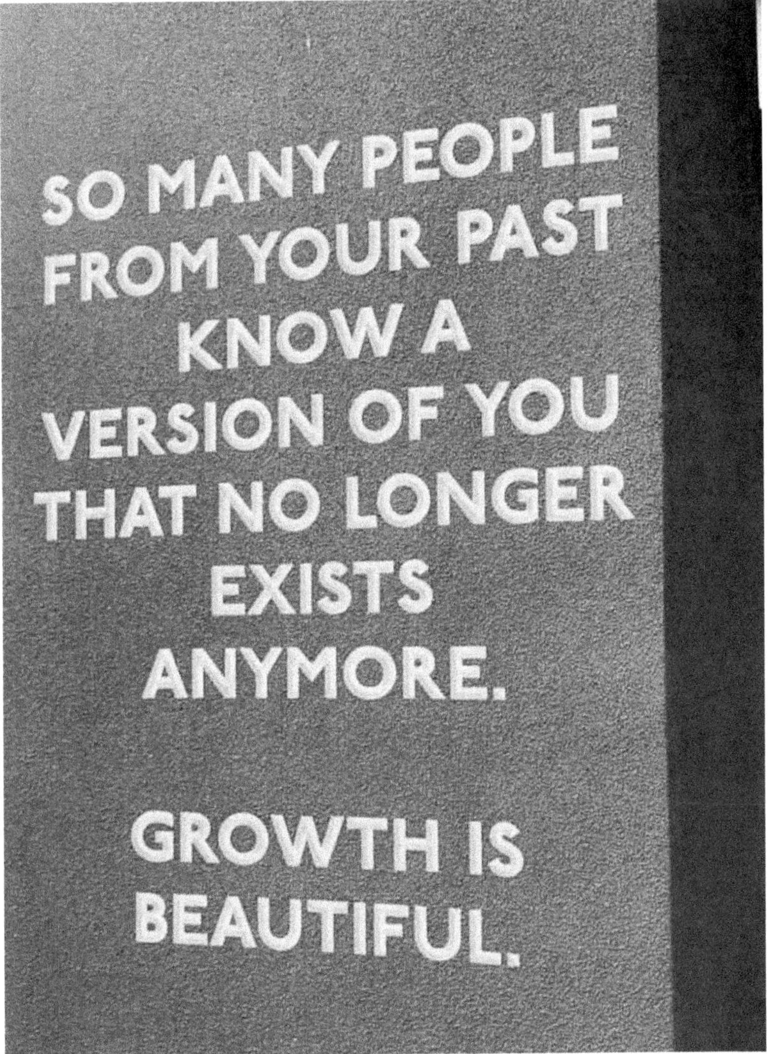


A priority for all readers. Happy Learning!